PROFESSIONAL
Portrait
TECHNIQUES

Kodak Publication No. O-4H

EASTMAN KODAK COMPANY • ROCHESTER, N.Y. 14650

©EASTMAN KODAK COMPANY, 1973
FIRST EDITION—FIRST PRINTING

LIBRARY OF CONGRESS CATALOG CARD NUMBER 72-95689
STANDARD BOOK NUMBER 0-87985-060-4

Kodak, Ektacolor, Vericolor, Estar, Versamat, Ektachrome, Kodacolor-X,
Ektachrome-X, Tri-X, Panalure, and Kodapak are trademarks.

5

original — the best portraitist is the one who combines in fullest measure the power of reading character, knowledge of the effects of light and shadow, and mastery of the techniques of his medium, and it necessarily follows that no one ever passes the need for study."

The dedicated portrait photographer never goes off duty. He practices his trade by studying faces wherever he is. He evaluates the natural lighting on the facial planes of the person across the aisle in a bus. He notes the spotlight effect on the waiter in the restaurant. He thinks in terms of light and shadow, and of contrast, as he studies the face of his next subject when they meet in the reception room. In the studio, before the sitting, he decides which of his subject's features he wants to emphasize before he even selects his props, camera, and lenses. Perhaps a fleeting smile or quick glance dictates a mobile camera, a fast shutter speed, and strong light. A quiet mood and serious expression could call for a secluded atmosphere, a large-format camera, with natural window light and reflectors. He should be diversified in his equipment so that he can be versatile in characterizing his subject.

The carefully controlled lighting and posing of the portrait can convey the intelligence, sensitivity, and strength of the subject, as well as his likeness. However, the candid approach to portraiture is helpful to characterization through association with familiar objects and places; the subject is at ease in familiar surroundings and thus is more natural in expression and pose. Bear in mind that the ordeal of having a formal portrait done is, to most people, one of the most agonizing of experiences. The photographer must do everything possible to eliminate this feeling of camera-shyness. One method is to place the sitter in the role of host, in his own home, or among the tools of his trade. The least a studio photographer can do to relieve his sitter's tension is to remove him mentally to familiar territory by finding a subject of conversation that he can elaborate upon until the proper expression is captured. Remember that the sitter's state of mind is reflected in his face. The photographer must be more concerned about his subject's feelings than about anything else.

Every person has a mental image of his own appearance, usually rather idealized. When he is at ease, in comfortable surroundings, and interested in what he is hearing and saying, his photographic image approaches the appearance of his mental image. This is the epitome of portraiture—capturing on film the likeness that matches the sitter's image of himself.

Future Direction

Today, the portrait photographer faces a crisis. The tools of his art are sophisticated and reliable. Another dimension—color—has made his images even more realistic and beautiful. But his customer has become accustomed to a world filled with photographic images which visually overwhelm, day and night. Pictures that move, talk, and shimmer with brighter-than-life color, created by masters of the camera.

What chance does the portrait stand in this cacophony of photographic advertising? Surprisingly enough, more chance than ever before, given a few creative opportunities. Human nature has not changed. Man is still primarily interested in himself and his own; therefore, portraits remain important to him. However, because he has been forcibly educated in the principles of design, color harmony, and composition by the advertising media, he will not accept the tired, static portraits so prevalent in the past. Perhaps, too, because he and his family do not stand still for very long today, those old-style pictures do not appear natural.

It has become necessary to start redesigning the portrait for tomorrow, keeping in mind the necessity for building growth into the portrait business today. To do this the portrait photographer must innovate as he works. He must accept or reject ideas, depending upon the reaction of his customers. He needs a never-ending flow of informational material on techniques and marketing. Much of this is now available, in one form or another, through the study of modern advertising photography methods, new art forms and uses of color, trends in current consumer publications; by attending seminars and workshops conducted throughout the photographic industry; and, finally, by supporting photographers' organizations that stress new ideas and new developments.

Technical Excellence

What Is Quality in Portraiture? This book is primarily a presentation of ideas for posing and lighting, but it is impossible to omit the mention of photographic quality in portraiture. A good photographic portrait is the sum of a number of different qualities: Lighting, composition, posing, your own individuality, and technical excellence are all parts of the whole. Each one is important, but in this chapter we dwell on the subject of technical quality because its absence can reduce the effectiveness of all the others. Good technical quality makes the difference between a drab portrait and one that "lives"—conveys the personality of the subject, or tells the story you intended it to tell.

By technical quality we mean the delicate gradation in highlights, the muted range of colors and tones in deep shadows, the rich scale of hues and values between light and shade, as well as the contrast, density, and color balance appropriate to the subject.

Quality in a portrait is usually obvious only when it's poor. If it's very good, then the observer sees only the subject; he is not conscious of the technicalities of photography. This is as it should be. People are interested in the subject of the portrait, not how the picture was obtained.

Art versus Technique: There is no conflict here. Some photographers feel that because they have an artistic touch, they are absolved from the task of understanding the technicalities of the medium. This way of thinking is a mistake; you are only part of the way to becoming an artist if you can't use your tools to express yourself competently. This is true of any creative activity, and it's particularly so in photography, where the technicalities are complex. The more you know about photographic materials and processes, the greater is your ability to use them to get the effect you want.

Negative Quality

No matter how imaginative or delicate your portrait lighting may be, it won't carry over into the print unless you pay attention to the factors in negative-making that influence image quality. These factors are (1) the camera lens and (2) the choice of film, exposure, and development.

The Camera Lens: To avoid unnatural size relationships in pictures of people, choose a lens of a longer focal length than you would normally use. A focal length of about 1½ or 2 times the diagonal of the negative is about right for a head-and-shoulders portrait, while a somewhat shorter focal length is adequate for three-quarter-length and full-length figures. The chart on page 11 gives suggested lens focal lengths and minimum working distances for various kinds of portraits taken in the studio.

Soft-Focus Lenses: Although the question of whether or not to use a soft-focus lens may be a matter of personal preference, most portraits are *not* made with sharp commercial lenses. Such lenses record every wrinkle, line, and blemish. As a result, the portrait is somewhat crude unless the sitter has practically flawless skin. Otherwise, an inordinate amount of skillful retouching may be needed to make the picture presentable.

Soft-focus lenses are specially designed to leave a moderate residue of spherical aberration. The effect of such aberration is to image a point, not sharply as with an ordinary lens, but with a halo of decreasing intensity around it. The effect is to diffuse and reduce the contrast of the fine detail in the image. Remember that putting the lens out of focus does not achieve this effect. With most soft-focus lenses, the amount of spherical aberration, and therefore the degree of softness, can be controlled either by stopping the lens down or by altering the separation between the component elements. Some older portrait lenses, however, relied on a measure of chromatic aberration to achieve softness. This type of aberration is not affected by reducing the lens aperture. If a soft-focus lens is not available, diffusing disks placed over the camera lens can be used to give a similar effect. Diffusing disks can also be used with an enlarging lens to achieve soft focus, but this method degrades the image and should only be used as a last resort.

Lens Care: Whether you use an old soft-focus lens or a modern, coated lens, it is essential to keep the glass surfaces clean. Dust, finger marks, and atmospheric grime cause an undesirable amount of flare, or non-image-forming light, to reach the film. (In addition, uncoated lenses may produce objectionable color fringing in color materials.) As a result, fine shadow detail is masked by fog and the contrast of highlight detail is lowered, sometimes to the point where it is nonexistent. Take care of your camera lenses and keep them covered when not in actual use. Constant cleaning with tissue or anything else eventually takes the high polish from the glass. Prevention is better than cure in this case.

Negative Exposure: Incorrect exposure of the negative is probably one of the main causes of poor quality in portrait photography. Too little exposure results in loss of shadow detail. In spite of increased development, in the case of black-and-white, the loss persists. A print from such a negative will almost certainly have shadow areas that are just plain black patches without detail to relieve them. A print from an underexposed color negative will not only be without detail in the shadows, but the shadows themselves usually will have a nasty green color that cannot be corrected in printing. Since the eye rarely sees detail-less shadows in a scene, they are objectionable in reproduction. Even dark, low-key prints need detail in the shadows.

Overexposure, on the other hand, produces several undesirable effects. The principal ones are a flattening, or a lack of gradation, in the highlights and a desaturation of color. These effects occur because overexposure places the highlights on that part of the characteristic curve of the film where exposure increases no longer record as density differences. The effect of overexposing the negative shows in the print as a single tone instead of gradation in the highlights. This is probably the most serious of all shortcomings in portrait photography. No matter how good your lighting is, overexposure destroys its effect,

and your prints are drab and lifeless. Other undesirable effects are increased graininess and loss of critical sharpness. Sharpness may not be particularly important for some portrait subjects, but it is of great importance for others where fine detail is desirable.

Correct Exposure and Exposure Latitude: The question is how to get correct exposure. Before answering it, a few words about exposure latitude are necessary. It has often been said that the exposure latitude of black-and-white films, and to a lesser extent of color negative films, is so great that you can vary exposure by several stops and still get a good negative. This statement is not quite correct. Since film speed numbers are based on the minimum exposure necessary to yield adequate shadow detail, there is little tolerance to underexposure. The amount of latitude you have to exposure greater than the desirable minimum depends on the brightness range, or more correctly, on the luminance ratio of the subject. A contrasty subject may have a ratio of about 130 to 1 or greater. A flat subject may have a ratio as low as 30 to 1. In practice, this means that you have less exposure latitude in photographing contrasty subjects than you have with flat ones that contain no important shadow areas. If you overexpose a subject with a high luminance ratio, the highlights may be recorded on the shoulder of the characteristic curve; as a result, they will be flat or some of the detail will be lost. Remember also that the high density resulting from overexposure increases graininess in the negative and reduces color saturation in the color print.

Film Speed: Film speed numbers, or exposure indexes, are related to the exposure needed to obtain a specified density at some point on the characteristic curve of the film. However, an exposure index does not stand alone outside the context of your particular photographic system. Any significant factor in the system can potentially alter the exposure index that is correct for you. Consequently, it's a good idea to check your black-and-

white exposure and development combination by making the ring-around described in the Data Book *KODAK Professional Black-and-White Films,* No. F-5.

The exposure indexes of Kodak color negative films require a fixed development time and temperature combination. However, an added variable is introduced into the photographic system by the color temperature of the light source. Individual color film types are designed to be used with light of a specific color temperature and must be filtered if the color temperature is varied. This, of course, changes the recommended exposure index. When possible, make test exposures and prints. See Kodak Data Book No. E-66, *Printing Color Negatives,* for a complete discussion of the color negative-positive system.

Use the Right Materials

There is a great deal of variety in both black-and-white and color film and paper products. It is therefore important to choose those that give the results you are seeking. Although many films and papers are versatile, generally one or two of them will be particularly suited to a given application. For information about choosing films and papers, see the Data Books *KODAK Professional Black-and-White Films,* No. F-5, *KODAK Black-and-White Photographic Papers,* No. G-1, and *KODAK Color Films,* No. E-77.

A Word to the Wise: Remember that anything at all that requires an artistic or a creative approach is subject to false starts, revised thinking, or a temporary deficiency of ideas. Never hesitate to say, "I don't like this result; I must do the job over again." If you don't like the picture, the chances are that other people won't like it either. You must be the judge, the jury—and the executioner; burn the print if it's not good enough. A poor photograph not only reflects directly upon its creator, but more importantly, lowers the status of photography as a whole.

Studio Portraiture

Traditionally, formal portrait sittings have taken place only in the studio. The necessity for skylights, large incandescent lamps, high-voltage power supply, unwieldy stands, and other specialized equipment dictated a special place for making photographs. Modern films, cameras, and light sources make these requirements obsolete, but the portrait studio, if suitably arranged, still remains ideally suited to its original purpose.

Today, the portraits produced in professional studios still dominate the field, both in quality and (except for school pictures) in quantity. There is a definite trend toward location and outdoor portraiture, but the photographers who travel to outside sittings need a home base in which to experiment and perfect their skills. The laboratory that is the professional studio will continue to be the birthplace of portraiture that is inventive and imaginative.

The Studio

It is a place away from distraction, where photographer and subject can be in harmony. It is a familiar place, comfortable to be in, with tested equipment that works without a flaw; where every possible variable in light and color is known and controlled; where the photographer, manipulating lights, camera, and subject, can progress from pose to pose without interruption, where the sitter is subjected to no unnecessary noises or surprises and can maintain his composure and privacy.

Because the portrait studio is still a special place, it should not be degraded. It is not a clubroom or a lunchroom. Keep the production staff out! The smell of stale cigarette smoke and salami sandwiches or the sudden appearance of shadowy forms beyond the modeling lights is not conducive to rapport with the sitter. It is not a storage area. Keep spare lights, posing benches, furniture, cameras, and backgrounds in a convenient anteroom, ready to be brought forth when needed between sittings or while the subject is in the dressing room. Make sure that the pathway to the posing bench is not an obstacle course. Arrange the equipment so that light stands, tripod, and particularly electric power cables are safely out of the way. Make every effort to see that your customer has a completely pleasant experience in your studio so that he will want to return.

Studio Size: The camera room should be spacious enough to move around in, with sufficient working space completely surrounding the posing bench.

An important dimension is the distance from the posing bench to the background. It should be enough so that no shadow from the subject will fall on the background, no matter how tall the subject is. This distance should also allow the background to fall out of sharp focus when the lens is stopped down to the working aperture.

There should be foreground room enough to use a lens of fairly long focal length and still cover a half-figure. And there should be plenty of room behind the camera to allow the photographer to move about freely.

The width of the studio should be such that both the main and the fill lights can move, in an arc around the subject to the background, without your changing the light-to-subject distances.

The floor space around the posing bench should be the most constantly used space in the studio. A portrait-lighting setup should not be static; that is, with lights placed in one spot, unmoved for sitting after sitting. Move the main and fill lights back and forth, as well as up and down, to create patterns and ratios of highlight and shadow on the contours of the subject's face until the effect most enhances his appearance. It follows that, since no two subjects are alike, no two lighting situations should be exactly the same.

Working Distances: The following chart was compiled to give the *minimum* studio working space needed to take a particular kind of portrait. Note that, with certain wide-field lenses, this minimum camera-to-subject distance can cause some subject distortion at the edges of the picture.

The final dimension to consider in the portrait studio is the ceiling height. It should be high enough to clear the hair-light boom and provide vertical

An Executive Studio Portrait

In a formal portrait like this, pose and camera height are used to help form an important psychological impression.

The subject is sitting in a relaxed position on the desk. He is an approachable, rather informal person. His arms and hands are spread wide apart, indicating an open, unsecretive nature. However, the camera is quite low, looking up with respect at the subject, who obviously is an important officer in his company.

The low-key background consists of several panels which are on casters and can be wheeled into several arrangements. A desk, chair, and some props complete the set.

Because the subject has a slim face and also because he has some character lines in his face, a simple, 3-to-1-ratio, broad-lighting arrangement is used, with a single hair light and one background light to illuminate the corner. Retouching is minimal.

Kodak Vericolor S Film 4105 (*Estar* Thick Base), 4 x 5-inch, was exposed in a view camera with an 8½-inch lens.

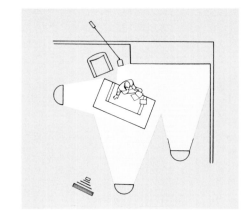

space for a background adequate for a standing figure, but low enough to be painted white and used as a bounce-light reflector for skylight effects. The consensus of portrait photographers is that a flat, white ceiling, free from beams and ductwork, is ideally located at a 12-foot height.

Whatever its size and location, the portrait studio is, above all, a workplace, productive and professional, containing everything needed to produce photographs that are technically and aesthetically worth purchasing.

Portrait Photography in Industry

Executive portraiture is one of the most important tools in the field of public relations. Good photographs of management people can help create a favorable public image for almost any corporation. A press release accompanied by a portrait of the individual involved stands a better chance of being picked up than one that doesn't. In fact, sometimes the picture can make or break the story. Color portraits, in the form of 35mm transparencies, are valuable visuals accompanying news releases to local TV stations. In another application, enlarged color portraits of leading executives can be used in a gallery strategically placed in public areas of the business office to create a corporate image of capable, dependable, and interested management. The executive gallery can be used to personalize board rooms, to impress and reassure customers in places of business, to make an exhibit at institutions the corporation has endowed, or to humanize the image of management in employee lounge areas.

WORKING DISTANCES

Film Size	Type of Portrait	Suggested Focal Length*	Minimum Working Space† (in feet)
35mm	Head and Shoulders	75mm	16
	Full-Length Figure	50mm	17
	Groups 10 Feet Wide	35mm	17
2¼ x 2¼ inches	Head and Shoulders	120mm	16
	Full-Length Figure	80mm	18
	Groups 10 Feet Wide	50mm	19
2¼ x 2¾ inches	Head and Shoulders	135mm	16
	Full-Length Figure	90mm	15
	Groups 10 Feet Wide	60mm	18
4 x 5 inches	Head and Shoulders	8½″ to 10″	15
	Full-Length Figure	6″	16
	Groups 10 Feet Wide	100mm (wide field)	18
5 x 7 inches	Head and Shoulders	12″ to 14″	15
	Full-Length Figure	8″ to 8½″	15
	Groups 10 Feet Wide	135mm (wide field)	16
8 x 10 inches	Head and Shoulders	14″ to 16″	15
	Full-Length Figure	12″	17
	Groups 10 Feet Wide	190mm (wide field)	18

*Not using camera swings.

†These values assume the image occupies 90 percent of the negative dimension and includes an allowance of about 7 feet for lights, background, and camera working room.

There are many other uses for photographs of a company's executives, too— the personnel department requires pictures of employees for record; the company magazine would like photographs to illustrate articles; each executive can carry his own photo business card that enables his business contacts to identify him readily; stockholders' reports are illustrated with pictures of top executives. The executive himself would probably welcome a color print of his own portrait for personal use. And his fellow workers might enjoy presenting him with a portrait upon retirement.

In many companies, the prime aim is to keep a file of fresh portraits by updating them periodically. As soon as an employee is elected to executive status, he is rushed to the portrait studio. At the sitting, both formal and informal poses, as well as pictures for the new executive's personal use, should be recorded. Both black-and-white and color film should be exposed (or provision for prints on KODAK PANALURE Paper should be available). Backgrounds and props should be simple and inconspicuous but should reflect something of the executive's personality or specialty. Whether the portrait is done in the studio, as on page 10, or on location in the business office, as on page 30, the emphasis remains on the individual, with the surroundings subdued by lighting or selective focus. Update sittings should be scheduled regularly. Retouching of negatives and prints should be minimal. Today, the public considers wrinkles and character lines actual symbols of status. A good executive is almost certain to have them. If he doesn't, it appears that he didn't have to work to attain his position.

Executive portraiture is an interesting and challenging field. The professional portrait photographer who recognizes this need of industry, or the industrial photographer who takes on the tasks of company public-relations portraiture, will find the work well worthwhile.

Studio Portrait Backgrounds

Generally, you should strive for simplicity in the background. Not only does simplicity yield more artistic results by maintaining the accent on the sitter, but it is a practical fact that the repeated use of a background with a definite or easily recognizable design quickly dates your work. Probably the most widely used background is a large, flat, unmarked surface. This can be paper (such as a large roll of seamless background paper, 9 feet wide, suspended from the ceiling), a painted screen, or an actual wall of the studio. To help prevent distracting reflections or color casts, paint with matte rather than glossy paint. By varying the relative amount of illumination on this background, you can easily control the overall tone, and you can introduce variations by throwing a shadow across an area of the background.

You can produce simple backgrounds without difficulty. They can be made of a piece of lightweight muslin stretched on a frame of ample size and painted with flat latex paint. Old tapestries make good backgrounds if used sparingly, as do bookcases and dark-toned plywood or paneled screens, especially for men. Incidentally, a posing platform about 8 inches high is an excellent aid in the portrait studio. It helps elevate the subject to a more convenient working height and, in addition, helps to eliminate the background floor line in three-quarter portraits.

Give the color of the background careful consideration. Backgrounds having large masses of one bright color are usually not suitable because they have a tendency to overpower the color likeness of the subject. An effective background might employ a soft cloud effect in which the colors are quite subdued. Slightly warm-colored backgrounds are suitable for most subjects, especially for low-key portraits. In general, avoid cold-colored backgrounds because they reflect from the sides of the face, giving a sickly look to the subject. Also, proper visual color balance is more difficult to achieve in printing a color portrait with a cold background because the complementary colors contrasting with warm flesh tones make the flesh appear excessively ruddy.

Painting a Studio Background: With a section of canvas, some paint, and no artistic training whatsoever, you can create a portrait background that will

Husband and Wife Portrait

After the executive portrait (page 10) was made, the opposite wall of the studio was utilized to produce this dual portrait. The background is a large painted canvas, blending to black at the edges. It is unstretched and rolls down the wall from a high bracket.

The lighting is predominately from the right of the picture, with only one weak fill light at the camera and some bounce from a white wall to the left. Note that the light-costumed woman is placed as far from the main lights as possible, while her dark-suited companion (with a darker complexion, as well) is close to the lights. The lighting ratio is approximately 5 to 1, which could be considered slightly high. However, the shadow side of the figures "breaks" nicely against the dark background.

An arrangement of chrysanthemums, to add a spot of color to the background, and a delicate French Provincial chair complete the simple props for the picture.

In all, a satisfactory and profitable second sitting in the appointment schedule of a busy executive.

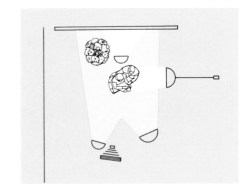

A Three-Quarter Portrait of an Elderly Lady

The translucent quality of this lady's skin, the soft wrinkles due to her years, and the sharp inquisitiveness of her eyes have been captured by using a large reflector as the only fill on the shadow side, and by taking advantage of the additional reflective qualities of her white shawl.

Two electronic flash units, one above the other, are used almost 45 degrees to the left of the camera. A small unit illuminates the background.

The background consists of a 9 x 12-foot oriental rug suspended from a rolling background flat.

Because of the sitter's tiny size, a posing platform 8 inches high is used to bring her up to proper camera height.

This exposure, on 4 x 5 *Kodak Vericolor* S Film 4105, was made during a particularly interesting conversation about northern New York State in the early nineteen hundreds.

result in photographs that are personal and distinctive. Because you do the painting yourself, you can alter the colors and densities until you are satisfied that they will harmonize properly with the subject.

You will need canvas from any awning store. The size will depend on your studio space. If there's plenty of space, you can find excellent use for a 12 x 12-foot canvas. This is suitable for full-length, large three-quarter, or family-group portraits. An 8 x 8-foot canvas can handle these categories, too, though with a group limit of three. For these sizes, mount the canvas on a simple frame of two-by-twos, and tack it into place. Add a set of rollers for mobility.

In these sizes, you may find there are seams. However, with the subject standing 5 or 6 feet in front of the background and with the lens of a 4 x 5 camera set at $f/8$ to $f/11$, seams don't show. The seam could be be a problem in a smaller studio where space does not permit this separation between subject and background—and here a window-shade-size canvas, suitably equipped to let you roll it up for storage, would be preferable.

You will need either water-based or oil-based colors for your background: water-based for a high-key (pale) background, the good semimatte for the darker low-key variety. Any reflections can be banished by applying an overcoat of flat varnish or by blending an additive with the paint to remove gloss. Or you can tilt the background slightly so that the highlights don't reflect back into the camera.

Your painting instruments are a roller, brush, sponge, and cloth. The roller and brush produce the harder lines and distinct patterns; if you're in a smaller studio, however, you'll want to skip them entirely. Larger studios, with room to maneuver the subject, can use them to advantage. Sponges and cloths are used to blend the design together, removing harsh contrast and providing a swirling "oil painting" look.

Keep the center of the canvas relatively pale—darkening as you move outward to the frame. This gives the portrait depth and separation, and it cuts down on the burning-in time later, too. A word of caution: Stay away from the

flesh tones while working the center, lest you camouflage your subject.

For low-key backgrounds, pick the earthen tones—brown hues, with additions of white, green, black, or red as required. Such backgrounds are good settings for adults, and for the more formal type of child and teen portraits. The high-key backgrounds are most effective for children in general and for fashion illustrations. Judge the finished background by viewing it through the ground glass with the camera focused *where the subject will be.*

How many backgrounds should you have?—literally as many as you can manage. The greater the variety of painted portrait settings available, the more versatile your service. You can find the right background for every subject, including the couple who arrive clad in unexpected hues, or the brunette who became a blonde between appointment and sitting. Three backgrounds— one high-key, two low-key—would be an excellent starting set. At an average cost of $20—plus paint, frame, and rollers—it is a modest investment.

Because it will increase your versatility, enrich your composition, and cut down on printing costs, you'll find the painted background a simple and serviceable addition to your studio.

Background Lighting: For the photograph to retain the same background color as you observe visually, the background must receive the same amount of illumination as the subject's face. For example, if the main light is 4 feet from the face, a light of equal intensity must be placed 4 feet from, and turned toward, the background. Position the subject 5 or 6 feet from the background in order to reduce the tendency for the spill from the main light to affect the background tone and color saturation. Do not rely on spill light to illuminate the background; *it should be treated as a separate subject. Light it independently.*

Two other excellent reasons for placing the subject at least 5 or 6 feet from the background are to prevent the background color from reflecting appreciably onto the subject and to allow background detail to go out of focus.

15

Background Lighting for High-Key Portraits: White backgrounds for high-key portraits can be very effective, and you can produce them easily by using on the background a light of sufficient intensity to yield a *background brightness four times that of the main subject.* Employing the same white background and reducing the strength of the background light to that of the main light is apt to produce greenish or bluish gray tones around the subject in the fall-off areas of the background.

In using white backgrounds for high-key portraits, there is considerable danger that excessive flare may cause a loss of picture contrast. To minimize this problem, photograph the background at a slight angle and make sure that the background is no larger than necessary. Use an efficient lens hood and black screens, just out of camera range, to minimize this image-destroying flare.

The Umbrella—A Portable Skylight

One of the greatest innovations in portrait photography in recent years is the soft lighting technique produced by the use of umbrellas. The photographic umbrella is remarkably similar to the "bumbershoot" used to protect the upper portion of a pedestrian from the elements; it consists of a metal shaft and a collapsible framework covered with cloth. Only the cloth covering differs. It is made of white or silvered material that is highly reflective. The light source

Girl in a Black Hat

This straightforward portrait is successful in spite of, or perhaps because of, a couple of broken rules. First, the body, head, and eyes are all directed straight at the camera, which is definitely considered static positioning. Second, the hand beneath the chin breaks the rule that a hand above the waist should be in an upward position. The selection of the pose was motivated by the dramatic inclinations of the young lady and her choice of clothing. Her face photographs best full front, emphasizing her expressive eyes. The sweep of her hair and hat are also best full front. Using her hands in this manner offsets the static positioning of the head and shoulders, and adds action to the pose. Finally, the dark green plant and olive-color background complement the bright red sweater.

The lighting consists of four electronic flash units: main light to the left, twin fill lights above and on both sides of the camera, and a background light low and behind the subject.

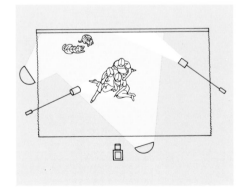

Informal Family Group Portrait

Mother and daughters are posed in a classical triangular composition. Using the oriental rug as a base and the oil-painted background (plus a couple of complacent ceramic tigers to complete the set), the photographer chose to use a Hasselblad camera with an 80mm lens in order to descend to floor level to capture this happy group on *Kodak Vericolor* S Film 120.

Note that the depth of field of the medium-format camera is much greater than that of the studio camera. The detail of the rug, props, and background might be considered distracting in a straight print. Here they have been burned-in.

This composition lends itself nicely to both full negative enlargement for wall decoration and, closely cropped, to wallet or desk-top prints for the man of the family.

—electronic flash, tungsten, or quartz lamp—is mounted on the shaft and aimed into the center of the underside of the parabolic framework. The quality of the light that is reflected from this surface is reminiscent of the soft, diffused, nondirectional light produced by the north skylight of early photographic studios. Here is a broad, natural-looking light source that is extremely portable.

The quality of skylight illumination varied from the soft dullness of a cloudy day to the relative sparkle of the sunny, clear sky, which produced definite shadows, even with light from the north. So, too, the quality of the umbrella light can be changed to match the mood of the subject. Umbrellas are available in a variety of shapes, sizes, and reflective qualities: 3 to 6 feet in size, square or round, flat or parabolic, matte or smooth, white or silvered. By changing the shape, reflective surface, or manner of mounting the light source, you can obtain a series of increasing contrasts.

1. The softest umbrella illumination is produced by a flat matte-white surface, with the light directed entirely toward the reflecting surface from as far down the shaft as possible.

2. You can achieve slightly more direction or contrast with a silvered, still flat umbrella.

3. More sparkle is added if the umbrella is a silver parabolic canopy, with light directed into it from the focal point on the shaft.

4. Still additional specularity can be created by using a bare bulb in the silver parabolic canopy. The effect here is toward a point source, softened by the additional light reflecting from the canopy.

Fill light is usually from another, more diffuse umbrella or from a flat reflector.

Beware of mixing white and silvered material in different umbrellas or reflectors when shooting color. The result of this type of mismatch is similar to mixing tungsten and daylight on the same negative—impossible to print.

Portrait of a Musician

The extreme close-up of this face was inspired by the size of the man as well as by his detailed features and good-humored expression. A saxophone player, he arrived at the studio dressed in a suit and tie. After several exposures, the photographer substituted the green turtleneck sweater and the blue dressing gown, then moved in for this close-up.

The horizontal format and close cropping further emphasize the textures and characterization.

Kodak Ektacolor Professional Film, Type S, was exposed at $f/5.6$ in an Imperial 90 camera with a roll-film back and a 10-inch diffused lens. Three 50-watt-second electronic flash units were used in a classic short-lighting arrangement.

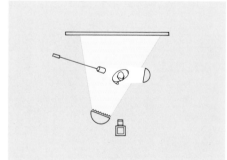

1890 Revisited

The swing of the fashion pendulum back to the styles of the past gives the photographer an opportunity to emulate the old-time masters of the wet plate, with an added ingredient—color.

Even the lighting resembles the broad skylighting of the old studios. The fill light consists of a bank of four electronic flash units in 16-inch reflectors bounced from a white ceiling. Another unit with a bubble diffuser, placed to the left of the camera, acts as the key light and also softens the shadows under the chins.

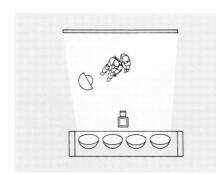

Girl with Harp

A broad fill light, a soft main light, and a kicker produce a pleasing study of a musician. The soft main light to the right of the camera provides a directional source, while the bank of four electronic flash units behind the camera produces a skylight-like fill. An undiffused unit far to the right rear picks up a highlight along the subject's neck, lightens her hair, and delineates the strings of the harp. A vignetter below the lens darkens the bottom of the picture.

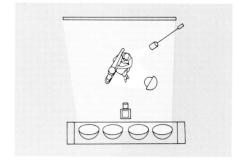

Girl with Rose

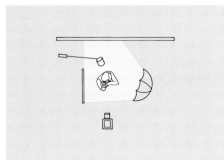

The young lady wanted "something different" for her boyfriend and was well pleased with this portrait.

The lighting setup is simple, with an umbrella-equipped electronic flash unit as a main source to the right of the camera, a white reflector as a fill, and a small flash unit high above as a hair light. The final print is cropped tightly for visual impact. The subject is a little on the plump side, but because of the pose, the use of short lighting, and the tight cropping, it doesn't show. Notice how the lighting arrangement, with no fill light at the camera, avoids problem reflections in the subject's glasses.

"Senior" Portraiture

The field of yearbook and senior portrait photography is a massive and lucrative one. As practiced by many photographers today, it is essentially an assembly-line production. If done with the proper equipment and good taste, however, the results are very pleasing.

These three photographs were made with the same practical lighting arrangement. However, the main light was not anchored in place, but was moved in an arc to the left of the camera as the changing situation demanded. A stationary fill light above the camera, a hair-light boom, and a weak background light completed the setup, giving a lighting ratio of approximately 4 to 1. The dark oil-painted background lends a three-dimensional quality. However, lighter backgrounds or more background illumination are sometimes demanded by yearbook editors.

These portraits were taken with a Hasselblad camera and an 80mm lens on *Kodak Vericolor* S Film 120. For this type of photography, a motorized camera is ideal—such as Camerez ID or a Beattie Portronic camera, with built-in identification provisions and accepting long rolls of 46mm or 70mm *Kodak Vericolor* S Film 2105 (*Estar* Base) or *Kodak Ektacolor* Professional Film 5026, Type S. Incidentally, these Kodak color negative films have "tooth" built into the base side to accept the retouching usually necessary in senior portraiture.

Young people who are finishing school and taking their place in society as wage-earners and consumers are your customers of the future. They are intelligent, sensitive, and have long memories. Treat them with respect!

Profile

This photograph typifies a great many of the young men of today. A close-up accentuates his serious mood as well as the lines created by the grooming of his beard and his glasses.

Three 50-watt-second electronic flash units are arranged in a simple split-light setup.

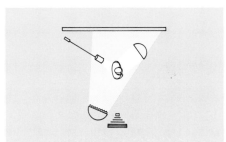

Informal Portrait of a Couple

Informality and naturalness are watchwords for today's younger adults. They like the way they look and want to be photographed that way. However, here is a portrait that is informal in dress and pose only. The lighting, set, and composition are most formal and exacting.

The lighting consists of two umbrellas (one on either side of the medium-format camera) about 6 feet high and reflecting down at a 45-degree angle. On the right side of the set, two more units are directed at the subjects (from almost a right angle) through a translucent diffuser made from a plastic shower curtain. On the left, a 4 x 5-foot reflector, made of 4 x 6-inch alternating gold and silver foil rectangles, serves as the only fill. A small hair light and a weak background light from above complete the arrangement.

The antique figured rug, the painted background, and the potted fern could have decorated a studio at the turn of the century. The guitar enjoys a renewed symbolism of freedom—not new, but not old.

The composition is broad-based, triangular, and static, but is relieved by the easy poses, harmonious colors, and pleasant expressions of the subjects.

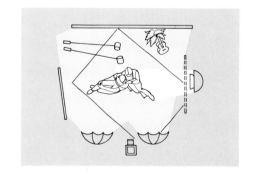

24

Full-Length Child Portrait

This lovely and serene six-year-old, seated in a miniature rocking chair, was photographed with a medium-format camera and *Kodak Ektacolor* Professional Film, Type S.

The lighting is a combination of a completely diffused umbrella main light, a small hair light and a directional background light. Note that the painted background is as highly lighted as the little girl's face, but because of its lack of detail and focus it does not fight for attention. The lighting ratio is low—about 2 to 1—and very appropriate for the subject.

Location Portraiture

For the professional photographer, the word "location" has meanings not dreamed of by Webster. From the depths of a diamond mine in Africa to the tip of Mount Everest and even to the Sea of Tranquillity on the moon, competent photographers have contended successfully with technical difficulties. However, for the purposes of this chapter, we will define location portraiture as photography done in an indoor place other than the portrait studio. (Thus the photographer may very well elect to use umbrella equipment on location, and if he uses electronic flash in the studio, he should find the material on that subject in this section helpful.) Outdoor portraiture, with its entirely different set of problems, is discussed in a later chapter.

The trials of location portraiture are similar to those of studio portraiture, but they are compounded by unfamiliar territory and logistics. The complete control of his surroundings enjoyed by the photographer in his own studio is missing. Low ceilings, small rooms, and cluttered furniture frustrate him in many instances. The inability to make and evaluate test exposures in advance of the sitting adds immeasurably to his mental strain. Finally, even with today's small-format cameras and compact speed-lighting equipment, the location-portrait photographer needs a station wagon, a strong back, and a fantastic memory to arrive at his destination completely equipped to do a professional job.

Why, then, is this type of portraiture becoming more and more popular? Primarily, because the public demands it. We are a society that is proud of its possessions. And we have more and richer possessions than ever before. What more natural inclination, when the need for a portrait is felt, than to wish to be photographed with your prized belongings? Now that it is technically possible, the smart photographer obliges —for an extra fee.

From the photographer's point of view, portraiture in the home, for all its inconveniences, produces very satisfying results. Since the subject is in familiar territory, expressions and attitudes are relatively more relaxed and natural. More importantly, the objects included in the photograph are not merely props but reflect the true personality of the sitter. (Be careful, however, not to make the picture one of a prized object, with its owner as a complementary subordinate.)

Location portraiture is not for the beginner. Full familiarity with equipment is essential, because seldom will it be used as conventionally as it is in the studio. Rapid placement of lights and reflectors (without measurements or tests) to obtain the lighting ratio necessary for proper reproduction takes the experience of many studio portrait sittings. The ability to recognize the dangers in color reflections from green or blue walls into flesh tones, or the futility of allowing light from mixed sources (fluorescent or tungsten with speedlight) to register on color film, comes from having viewed the results of many similar disasters—and having to retake the shots.

Location portraiture may be an expensive undertaking for the photographer because of the travel time and cost, as well as the outlay for specialized equipment. Therefore, it must be relatively more expensive for the customer. Make sure that the quality of the resulting pictures is worth this extra expense. If possible, visit the location before the day of the sitting. Plan where the subject will locate and what will be included in the picture. Mentally plan the position of the lights, or make a rough sketch of the floor plan. Locate electrical outlets. (It's better to have speedlight units with their own power supply.) Investigate the possibility of using existing natural light. In discussing the portrait session with the sitter, insist that he plan to devote the required time exclusively to the sitting, without distraction or interruption. You will find that extensive planning will pay off in better, more professional photographic results. Start the actual sitting with simple sets and basic lighting. Don't experiment at first. Gradually increase the complexity of the setup as the sitting progresses, and finish by recording the unusual situations that often present themselves. By proceeding in this deliberate manner, you will find that your subject, when he sees the proofs,

Couple by a Fountain

The location for this portrait is the fountain court of the Memorial Art Gallery of the University of Rochester. This medieval great hall—80 feet long, 40 feet wide and three stories high—is illuminated by rows of windows along the ceiling as well as by a huge wrought-iron chandelier containing incandescent bulbs. Usually, this mixture of light sources causes nothing but trouble for color photographs. In this case, however, the huge size of the set enables it to act as an integrating sphere for the two light sources, making an acceptable mixture. Because they are all of warm hues, the ancient Italian fountain, the French tapestry, and the terrazzo floor do not fight the balance of the light sources. The resulting blend of colors is very complimentary to the flesh tones of the subjects.

The lighting for the subjects consists simply of two electronic flash units—one at the camera, and one high and far to the left—in a strong 4-to-1 lighting ratio. The camera is a Hasselblad camera with an 80mm lens. The film is *Kodak Vericolor* S Film 120.

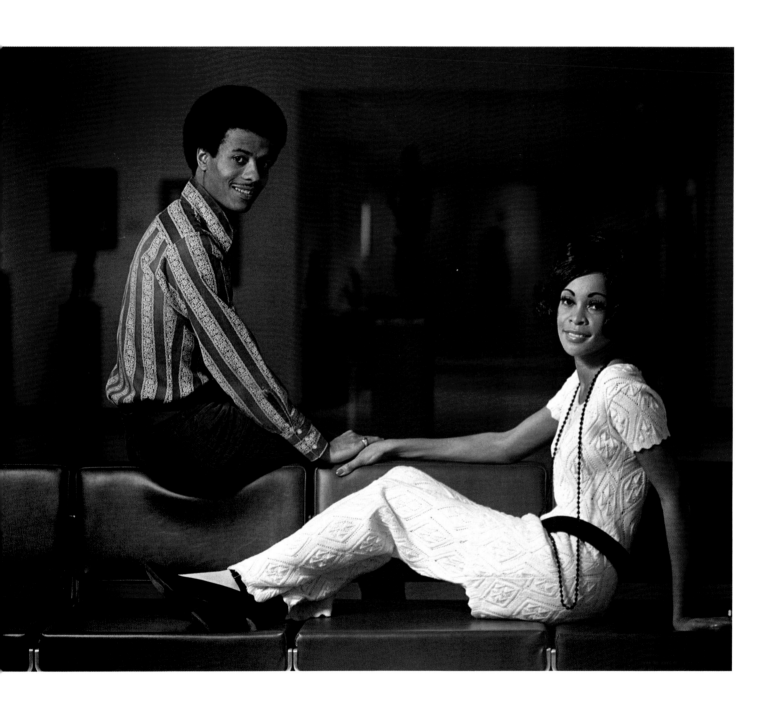

Guide Numbers for Electronic Flash

| SPEED | | OUTPUT OF ELECTRONIC FLASH UNIT (ECPS or BCPS) | | | | | | | | | | | | | | | | | | | |
| | | 350 | | 500 | | 700 | | 1000 | | 1400 | | 2000 | | 2800 | | 4000 | | 5600 | | 8000 | |
DIN	ASA	Feet	Meters	F	M	F	M	F	M	F	M	F	M	F	M	F	M	F	M	F	M
11	10	13	4	16	5	18	5.5	22	6.5	26	8	32	10	35	11	45	14	55	17	65	20
12	12	14	4	18	5.5	20	6	24	7	28	8	35	10.5	40	12	50	15	60	18	70	21
13	16	17	5	20	6	24	7	28	8	32	10	40	12	50	15	55	17	65	20	80	24
14	20	18	5.5	22	6.5	26	8	32	10	35	11	45	14	55	17	65	20	75	22	90	27
15	25	20	6	24	7	30	9	35	11	40	12	50	15	60	18	70	21	85	26	100	30
16	32	24	7	28	8	32	10	40	12	50	15	55	17	65	20	80	24	95	29	110	33
17	40	26	8	32	10	35	11	45	14	55	17	65	20	75	22	90	27	110	33	130	40
18	50	30	9	35	11	40	12	50	15	60	18	70	21	85	26	100	30	120	36	140	42
19	64	32	10	40	12	45	14	55	17	65	20	80	24	95	29	110	33	130	40	160	50
20	80	35	11	45	14	55	17	65	20	75	22	90	27	110	33	130	40	150	46	180	55
21	100	40	12	50	15	60	18	70	21	85	26	100	30	120	36	140	42	170	50	200	60
22	125	45	14	55	17	65	20	80	24	95	29	110	33	130	40	160	50	190	60	220	65
23	160	55	17	65	20	75	22	90	27	110	33	130	40	150	46	180	55	210	65	250	75
24	200	60	18	70	21	85	26	100	30	120	36	140	42	170	50	200	60	240	70	280	85
25	250	65	20	80	24	95	29	110	33	130	40	160	50	190	60	220	65	260	80	320	95
26	320	75	22	90	27	110	33	130	40	150	46	180	55	210	65	250	75	300	90	360	110
27	400	85	26	100	30	120	36	140	42	170	50	200	60	240	70	280	85	340	105	400	120
28	500	95	29	110	33	130	40	160	50	190	60	220	65	260	80	320	95	370	110	450	135
29	650	110	33	130	40	150	46	180	55	210	65	260	75	300	90	360	110	430	130	510	155
30	800	120	36	140	42	170	50	200	60	240	70	280	85	330	100	400	120	470	143	560	170
31	1000	130	40	160	50	190	60	220	65	260	80	320	95	380	115	450	135	530	161	630	190
32	1250	150	46	180	55	210	65	250	75	300	90	350	105	420	125	500	150	600	180	700	210
33	1600	170	50	200	60	240	70	280	85	340	105	400	120	480	145	560	170	670	205	800	244

◀ *Couple in a Gallery*

A composition in warm tones. The 19th and 20th Century French Gallery of the Memorial Art Gallery is the setting for this relaxed modern couple. The subjects are illuminated with two electronic flash units—one high and to the left of the camera and one at the camera. The background is illuminated with the existing tungsten museum lights. In this case, the mixture of two light sources enhances the photograph by warming the background tones to harmonize with the subjects' flesh tones. The blue-gray color of the modern couch contrasts nicely with the surrounding warm tones.

will choose the photographs he is attracted to by his personal degree of sophistication. Since all of the pictures contain familiar elements, chances of immediate acceptance of more than one of the poses are greatly heightened.

The proficient location-portrait photographer will find that his rewards mount amazingly. Word-of-mouth advertising of good work spreads rapidly. The craftsman who plans carefully and achieves technical perfection, as well as character delineation, will work to a full schedule in a most interesting field.

Proper Exposure with Electronic Flash

Exposure with electronic flash is based on the distance from the flash unit to the subject. To determine the correct camera settings, proceed as you do when using flashbulbs—divide the guide number by the distance from the flash unit to the subject. There are two differences, however; (1) with electronic flash, the guide number for a given film is the same at any shutter speed; (2) usually the guide number must be determined by the photographer's tests of his own equipment rather than by consulting a printed chart.

The guide number is the same at any shutter speed because the duration of the electronic flash is so short that even the fastest shutter speeds will catch the complete light output when the shutter is properly adjusted at X synchronization. (Focal-plane shutters usually must be set at no faster than 1/60 second with electronic flash.)

The photographer must test his own equipment when using electronic flash, because the light output of an electronic flash unit depends on several things: the energy applied to the flashtube (measured in watt-seconds), the efficiency of the tube, the efficiency of the reflector, and the number of flash units being fired from a single power source.

You can get greater flexibility of lighting control by using more than one light, just as in any method of lighting. However, you cannot increase the total output of light when you use extension electronic flash units on the same power pack. Two lights from one power pack will produce no more light than a single light from one power pack, but two units on one power pack do cut the flash duration in half.

Many manufacturers of electronic flash equipment furnish only the watt-second output of their power packs. It is up to the photographer to determine the actual amount of light, measured in beam candlepower seconds (BCPS), that his particular combination of power pack, flashtube, and reflector delivers. The only practical way to do this is to make tests. Use a roll-film camera loaded with a reversal color film, such as KODAK EKTACHROME-X Film (ASA 64). Place a subject *exactly* 10 feet from the flash unit, in surroundings similar to your normal backgrounds. Using the recommended shutter speed for your camera and flash unit, make a series of exposures at half-stop intervals. For the mid-point in the series, use the lens opening

Executive Portrait (on Location)

Since a 30 x 40-inch color print had been presold, a 5 x 7 camera (with a 10-inch lens stopped down to between f/8 and f/11) is employed to photograph this executive in his office. The subject is seated on the edge of his desk, about 10 feet from the background. Two 45-inch electronic-flash equipped umbrellas of 200 watt-seconds each are used for illumination. The fill light is 9 feet from the subject, to the left of the camera, and the main light is 5 feet away to the right. There are no hair or background lights. The objects on the desk and background are rendered out of focus by the shallow depth of field at this f-stop.

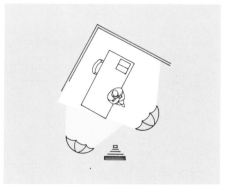

you think is correct for your film and flash combination. (A rough estimate is that a 100-watt-second unit delivers about 1,500 to 2,000 BCPS, a 200-watt-second unit, 3,000 to 4,000 BCPS, etc.) In each exposure, display a card marked with the *f*-stop used. Finish the roll of film by exposing the remaining frames on the same subject in full sunlight. Use an exposure meter to evaluate the exposure. Under normal viewing conditions, pick the processed transparency with the best exposure as compared with the outdoor frames. Multiply by 10 the lens opening used to make that exposure. The answer is your guide number for that combination of film and flash.

Once you have the guide number for one kind of Kodak film, you can find the guide number for any other film by using the table on page 29. Find your guide number opposite the ASA rating you used for the test. Any of the guide numbers listed in the same vertical column will work for your equipment and for other conventional films with listed ASA ratings.

Divide the guide number by the distance from the flash unit to the subject to determine the proper *f*-stop to use.

Incidentally, at the top of that column is the BCPS rating of your electronic flash unit.

Bridal Close-Up

The warmth of her home and the lovely objects dear to her surround this bride in her wedding portrait. Selective focus centers attention upon her face, while the softly defined, colorful carafes frame the picture.

Natural window light furnishes the main source of illumination, while a tiny 2-watt-second flash unit, mounted on the lens shade, fills the shadows. The camera is a medium-format single-lens reflex with a 150mm lens. The film is *Kodak Ektacolor* Professional Film, Type S (CPS), 120.

A Three-Quarter Male Portrait

Precisely proper negative exposure is essential to maintain the tonal differentiation between this subject's dark blue blazer and the black anteroom containing 13th-century French stained-glass window medallions. The medallions are backlighted with fluorescent tubes, adding the problem of mixed light sources to the task of balancing the intensity of the electronic flash with the transmitted light from the stained glass. The lighting consists of one unit at the camera and one unit so far to the right as to be almost rim-lighting the subject. *Kodak Vericolor* S Film 120, in a Hasselblad camera with an 80mm lens, is the color negative material used. Note the highlight detail as well as the shadow contrast. The film is processed in a *Kodak Versamat* Color Processor, Model 145.

A Full-Length Executive Portrait

This simple photograph, made without props or artificial lights, is an effective portrait because the camera height, pose, and cropping work together. The chest-high camera position adds stature to the figure, which stands three-dimensionally on the perspective point of the long hallway. All lines lead to the subject's head, directing the viewer's gaze to the eyes. The close, vertical cropping relates the figure to the edges of the print and eliminates all distractions.

Soft skylighting, through the floor-to-ceiling windows on the left, and reflection from the white wall on the right are the only illumination.

Mother and Children at Home

This is a very conventional approach to portraiture in the home. In a situation like this—with children, babies, and pets—it is most important to compose the picture and light it before placing the subjects. By creating the setting first, then introducing the subjects into it, you can rely upon their responding naturally and still keep the situation under your control. The resulting picture is then convincing rather than being overly contrived.

Two electronic flash units in polished 9-inch reflectors are the main light source to the right of the camera. Two more units in 16-inch satin-finished reflectors, on either side of the camera, are the fill lights. The photograph was made on *Kodak Ektachrome* Film 6115, Daylight Type (Process E-3), 4 x 5-inch. Dye transfer prints were delivered to the customer.

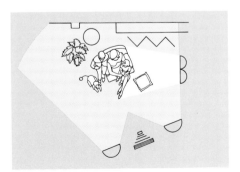

◀ Bridal, Three-Quarter Length

An impressionistic painting, a ceramic figurine, and an extremely low contrast ratio lend a modern feeling to this pastel bridal portrait.

The main light source is a large, curtained window behind the camera, which casts an almost shadowless light on the scene. A small electronic flash on the camera adds specular highlights.

Girl with Animals

The concept here is to show the emerging young personality, still almost tomboy, but with a very feminine aura. The easy composition was a simple matter of discovery upon entering the room. Finding the props was no problem.

Use of window light conventionally indicates the primary direction of light in the picture. In this case, the usual rule is impossible, for the subject would be in darkness. To retain as much feeling as possible of sunlight coming through draperies of another window and falling on the rug, two electronic flash units in polished 9-inch reflectors are placed high and far to the left of the camera. The fill consists of two units in 16-inch reflectors bounced off the ceiling from positions on either side of the camera. A 4 x 5-inch view camera with a 7½-inch lens was used to expose *Kodak Ektacolor* Professional Film, Type S.

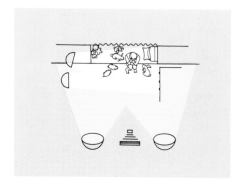

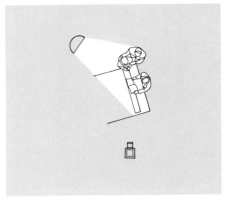

Bar Mitzvah

Two photographs showing the love of one generation for another.

The picture of the boy with his grandfather holds much meaning. They are together and deeply involved with one another.

When you are working with natural light coming from one side, photographing two people facing each other is often difficult, because one face necessarily goes into deep shadow. In this case, however, the location is outdoors, under a porch roof. The subjects are close to the edge of the roof, so enough light comes from the sky to fill the shadows.

The picture of the boy reading the Torah is a dramatic example of single flash. One electronic flash unit, placed far to the left of the camera in an extreme split-light position, is the only added source of illumination. There is no sky light here to fill the shadows. But notice how the light reflecting from the mother's flowers and the son's vestments adds detail exposure in the heavily shadowed areas. In printing and retouching, the extreme highlights were reduced on the parents' faces.

36

Bride and Groom

Careful posing, natural window light, and attention to detail make a deceptively simple looking photograph successful.

The bride admires her bouquet while her groom gazes at his new wife. A classic situation. But notice that the groom is positioned so that the bride's profile is clearly outlined. Her body is turned to the camera to give adequate support to her head and to delineate the detail of her gown. The composition is carefully arranged to avoid distracting background details. The exposure, 1/30 sec at f/2.8, affords a shallow depth of field which allows the groom to go "sentimentally soft," thus centering interest on the bride.

The main light comes from a window, carefully cropped from the left of the picture; a silver reflector fills the shadows.

Flower Girl and Groom

The idea behind this sensitive study is to show a closeness between the little girl and the man. Interest in the flowers is natural for her, while he looks on. Again, we are trying to show people at a wedding who are involved with what is going on, rather than posing for the photographer. The appearance is that the photographer just happened to be there to capture this brief moment.

Exposure was made by daylight, coming through a small window about 3 feet to the right of the subjects. A silver reflector, just out of camera range, supplies fill illumination. Exposure time was 1/30 sec at f/5.6, judged by meter.

Basic Lighting for Portraiture

This chapter will be concerned with some of the conventional lighting techniques used by professional photographers on a day-to-day basis to produce artistic and salable likenesses of their customers. These are, for the most part, basic lighting methods. Consider them stepping-off points for your own innovations.

To some readers, these procedures may be a form of review; yet perhaps a suggestion here or there might help them correct a lighting flaw that has remained unnoticed. Perhaps a method will suggest a new way to more efficient camera-room techniques or more artistic results.

Hopefully, the newcomer to photography, or the commercial or industrial photographer called upon to make an occasional portrait, will use this material as a primer in learning basic portrait lighting.

Definitions

The goal of the portrait photographer is to idealize his subject. His tools in achieving this end include the pose, camera angle, lighting, and retouching—but of all of these, the most pliable is the lighting.

The proper lighting can create modelling and realism: using the concept that light areas of a print project and dark areas recede, place highlights on the five frontal planes of the face (forehead, nose, chin, and both cheeks) with the neck and sides of the face in shadow. This helps lend a desirable third-dimensional effect to the subject.

Equally important, the lighting can be used to idealize: facial defects can be obscured in a shadow; a broad nose can be narrowed with a short lighting of the "split" variety.

Probably the most basic single principle governing portrait lighting (as well as product photography) is that there should be *One Dominant Light Source,* with all other lights subordinate and subservient to it. Accordingly, the character and placement of the main, or key, light in relation to the position of the subject is of primary consideration to the portrait photographer. Its placement is used as a means of classifying the three main types of lighting as follows:

1. Broad Lighting. The main light illuminates fully the side of the face turned *Toward* the camera. Although this lighting helps to de-emphasize facial textures, it is used primarily as a corrective lighting technique to help widen thin or narrow faces.

2. Short Lighting (sometimes known as "narrow" lighting). The main light illuminates fully the side of the face turned *Away* from the camera. This lighting is generally used for the average oval face of either a man or a woman. It tends to emphasize facial contours more than broad lighting and, in conjunction with a comparatively weak fill-in light, can be used as "strong" or "masculine" lighting especially adaptable for low-key portraits. Short lighting has the effect of narrowing the face and, therefore, can be used effectively as a corrective lighting technique for round or plump faces.

3. Butterfly Lighting. The main light is placed directly in front of the face and casts a nose shadow directly underneath, and in line with, the nose. Butterfly lighting is used most successfully with a normal oval face and is considered a type of glamour lighting especially suitable for young women. It is not usually suggested for men because of the way in which the subject's ears might be highlighted and made undesirably prominent.

Lighting Variations

Bounce Light: From these three basic lighting positions for the main light, any number of derivations can be achieved. From the broad lighting position *Bounce Light* is derived. This is accomplished by aiming the main light *Directly Away* from the subject to a suitable reflector. The light that is reflected to the subject is soft, shadowless, and most flattering. Often no fill-in light is used, or perhaps only further bounce from another reflector on the far side of the subject to soften the shadows.

Direct Light: Another derivation from the broad lighting position is so-called direct light. The main light in direct

Broad Lighting

Short Lighting

Butterfly Lighting

lighting is a high, reflectorless unit which throws an all-over sun-like illumination on the subject. Usually directed on the side of the subject turned toward the camera, the direct light is more directional than bounce light and gives more highlight separation. Fill-in is accomplished by an auxiliary light source or large reflectors.

Window Light: A popular use of the short lighting position is window light. Usually a combination of daylight and auxiliary electronic flash, it produces a natural, soft, low-key portrait. The subject is placed beside a window lit by skylight, not direct sunlight. The fill-in unit is on or near the camera and is one-half or less the intensity of the window light. If you are shooting with color film, be careful that the color temperature of your fill-in light agrees with the daylight coming in the window. (Photographic daylight is considered to be 5500 K.)

Split Light: The main light can be moved far enough behind the subject so that only half of the face is highlighted and there is no triangular patch of light on the nearest cheek. This variation of short lighting, known as "split" lighting, is used only rarely, and then to produce moderately dramatic low-key effects, conceal facial defects in the shadow side of the face, or slenderize a very broad nose.

Ceiling Bounce: One of the most widely used forms of bounce lighting, where the electronic flash unit is on camera and pointed directly up, automatically gives the results of a softened *Butterfly Lighting Position*. Once again, fill-in can be accomplished by reflectors placed horizontally under the subject's chin, or by white floors.

Drawbacks to this form of *Butterfly Lighting* are the necessity for white ceilings and the lack of specular highlights in the photographic subject's eyes. (A 3 x 5-inch card, taped to the flash head, will receive some light from a unit aimed at the ceiling, and this will add sparkle to eyes. It will also relieve shadows caused by eyeglasses.) However, used with a reflex-type camera, ceiling bounce is an ideally portable illumination for following a small child in a high-key studio.

These are only a few variations of the three basic lighting positions of the main light. Of course, to do a professional portrait with one light is possible, and it is often done to achieve a special effect. Normally, however, a portrait photographer uses a number of lights to build a suitable lighting for the subject. While no two photographers proceed in exactly the same way, you should follow an efficient, consistent operating method of adding lights to a portrait set. The list of individual lights might be the following, in this order:

Background Light

1. The Background Light. Customarily, the background light is a small flood lamp on a short stand placed about midway between the subject and the background. Its purpose is to help provide tonal separation between the subject and the background and, when color film is used, to control the color and general rendition of the background. Although it is a matter of personal preference, some photographers start the lighting buildup by adjusting the position of the background light. Exact placement of this light can be achieved more easily when its effect can be observed by itself.

Placement of the background light is facilitated if the photographer will first direct it *Toward the Subject,* watching the shadow the modelling light casts. The subject's shadow should completely cover the camera, thus making sure that the lens will not see any part of the background light itself. The background light is then rotated 180 degrees, and final placement adjustments are made.

2. The Main Light. Generally, this is a flood lamp or broad light source located higher than the subject's head and at approximately 45 degrees to one side of the camera-subject axis, usually in the short-light position. One method of placing this light properly, using the modelling lights, is to *Watch the Resultant Catchlights in the Eyes.* As seen from the camera-lens position, these catchlights should be located at approximately the 1 o'clock or 11 o'clock position in the eyes, depending on whether broad or short lighting is used and on the direction the subject is facing. Obviously, these catchlight locations will vary somewhat from subject to subject. For example, for a person with deep-set eyes or a person wearing a wide-brimmed hat, the main light will have to be lowered somewhat from the normal. However, the important point is that the main light must cause catchlights high in the eyes; otherwise (if it's too high, for instance), the eye sockets will appear to be excessively dark and recessed. About the only reason for using the main light very high would be to emphasize forehead wrinkles as much as possible, as in character-study work. Obviously, this won't do for day-to-day, salable studio portraits.

Most photographers use a diffused main light because a sharp shadow from the main light is not so desirable in portraiture as it is in commercial product photography. Diffused lighting minimizes facial textures, helps to minimize retouching, and, accordingly, is used most often for conventional portraits of both men and women. As a matter of personal preference, a few photographers use an undiffused main light for men, to accentuate character lines in the face or to produce a brilliant glamour effect. But this lighting is more difficult to control and would be used more for

A normal, oval face and conventional short lighting. Note that the main light has been positioned laterally so that it places a triangular highlight on the cheek nearest the camera.

A wider-than-normal face. In order to make it appear more normal, the main light has been moved further to the left and the width of the triangular highlight reduced.

Highlighting a comparatively greater area of a narrow face can make it appear somewhat wider. Thus, the width of the highlighted area of the face in any portrait should be about equal, regardless of the facial type.

special effect or salon results than for bread-and-butter portraits.

The next question to be answered is, should you use short or broad lighting? Discounting personal preference, the subject's facial structure provides the answer. The average oval face is presented most flatteringly with short lighting; the broad face, also with short lighting; and the narrow face, with broad lighting. The above diagram illustrates these three basic situations.

Note that the width of the highlighted area for all three subjects is approximately the same. The lighting has been designed to idealize the narrow and the broad faces and present them as normal. The basic consideration is that the broader the face, the more of it should be kept in shadow; and, conversely, the narrower the face, the more of it needs to be highlighted. It is for this reason that the triangular highlight on the broad face is intentionally smaller than the equivalent area on the normal face. The reduction of this cheek highlight is accomplished, of course, by moving the main light slightly farther behind the subject. This is a delicate adjustment. Its effect can be judged accurately *Only* from the camera lens position.

Broad lighting, used less frequently than short lighting, requires additional care and skill. The broad position of the main light means that too great a portion of the near side of the subject's face, including the ear, will be highlighted excessively. To keep this area in shadow, some means of controlling the distribution of light must be used. This shading can be accomplished by means of feathering, barn doors, or head screens. Obviously, a combination of these methods can be used.

3. The Fill-in Light. Generally, the fill light is diffused, used close to the camera at lens height, and placed on the side of the lens opposite that of the main light. Some slight modification of this position may be necessary for people wearing glasses, to avoid reflections.

The lateral position of the fill light is determined to some extent by the specular facial highlights this light causes. *The Effect Must be Observed Carefully from the Lens Position.* If, for example, a person has a type of skin that reflects the image of the fill light too strongly when the light is right next to the camera, these specular highlights can be reduced by moving the fill light slightly away from

Short Lighting (main light only)

. . . add the fill light

the camera. Often, this lateral adjustment is critical in controlling the degree of highlight brilliance and, as mentioned before, *the Effect Must be Carefully Observed from the Lens Position.*

Another consideration in the lateral position of the fill light is that undesirable shadows caused by smile lines may be created by using this light too far from the camera.

Almost inevitably, the fill light will add a lower pair of catchlights to the eyes. These secondary catchlights are usually considered objectionable, not so much because they tend to belie the basic principle of one main light source, but because they often create the impression that the subject has a directionless stare (a starry-eyed effect). Consequently, this second pair of catchlights should be removed. This can be done either by etching them in the negative (if a black-and-white film was used) or, more easily, by spotting them on the print (which can be done on either black-and-white or color prints). Color negatives cannot be etched successfully, due to the color-layer structure of the emulsion.

. . . add the background light

. . . add the hair light

. . . finally, add the kicker lights on both sides

Be sure to check the section, "Lighting Ratio," on page 44 for additional information regarding exact placement of the fill-in light.

4. The Hair Light. This small lighting unit, generally used on a boom from above and behind the subject, is almost a necessity. It not only adds some detail to the reproduction of the hair but also provides a useful means of subject-background separation.

There are three general positions relative to the subject where the hair light can be used effectively: directly overhead, either to the right or the left of his hair at head level, or above and to one side of him. In any case, the hair light should seldom be allowed to spill over onto the face, since this may cause small but distracting highlights and belie the basic principle of a single light source. A suggestion for placing the hair light properly is to bring it forward gradually until its illumination just strikes the forehead or the cheeks, as the case may be, and then move it back until the highlight on the skin disappears.

Broad Lighting (main light only)

. . . add the fill light

. . . add the background light

. . . add the hair light

. . . finally, add the kicker lights on both sides

43

Aside from the photographer's personal preference as to the rendering, the color and, especially, the degree of sheen of the hair dictate the amount of hair illumination required. Brunette hair requires more intense illumination than blond; dull hair, regardless of color, requires a relatively intense hair light in order to restore a desirable sparkle. The actual intensity is something that cannot be learned from a book—it is a matter of recognizing an artistic visual balance in the studio.

5. The Backlight. Often referred to as a "kicker," the backlight finds most use in outlining the shoulders of men's dark suits, to separate them from dark backgrounds. It's also helpful in adding detail to hair and, in rare instances of dramatic portraits, as a facial backlight. This lighting unit, generally a spotlight, is used slightly above the height of the subject's head and usually, but not always, on the same side of the subject as the main light. If used properly—better too little than too much—and from the same side of the subject as the main light, it can help add strength to a masculine face when it rims or grazes the extreme edge of the face. When the backlight is used on the opposite side from the main light, it often creates an undesirable effect by outlining the ear and making it appear to pull away from the head.

A precaution in using the backlight is that it usually should not be allowed to strike the tip of the subject's nose. If it does, it may give an abnormal appearance to the nose. Just a slight repositioning of either the light itself or the subject's head can prevent this lighting error. Be sure that both the hair light and the backlight are turned off when taking an exposure-meter reading. Not only do these lights have no effect on the basic exposure, but the danger is that they may influence the meter incorrectly. And, of course, no backlight should shine directly into the camera lens, since this might cause glare which would reduce the image contrast. A "barn door" or "snoot" can be used to shield the lens from this spill light.

Lighting Ratio

"Lighting ratio" refers to the relative intensities at the subject position of the

A "feathered" light refers to the fact that the subject is illuminated by the peripheral area of the light cone. Generally, the light is feathered in such a way that the reflector axis is in front of the subject.

In a broad-lighting situation, an alternate method of shading the nearest ear is to use the barn-door baffle attached to the lamp reflector. Barn doors are also useful in shading white blouses or bald heads.

A head screen has the advantage of more positive shading control since it can be used independently of the subject. Two screens will be useful as studio accessories.

main light plus the fill-in light to the fill-in alone. Generally, for normal contrast in portraits, the ratio should be in the neighborhood of 3 to 1. *This Ratio Will Produce Good, Salable Portraits for Both Black-and-White and Color Photography*. The apprehension that there is something different or mysterious about the lighting for a color portrait is groundless if a normal lighting ratio is maintained. Perhaps this feeling

stems from the fact that in black-and-white portraiture a high lighting ratio, say even 8 to 1, can be partially remedied by printing the negative on a low-contrast grade of paper. However, in color photography there is only one grade of paper available, and the principal method of contrast control is the establishment and maintenance of a consistent 3-to-1 lighting ratio by the photographer.

In general, a 3-to-1 ratio is achieved when, as measured at the subject, *The Main Light is Twice as Bright as the Fill-in Light When the Fill-in Light is Used Close to the Camera Lens.* This is because the fill light from the front places one unit of light over the *Entire* face, while the main light from the side (being twice as intense) places two units of light *Only* on the main-lighted areas of the face. Thus, there is only one unit of light in the shadows, but one plus two (that is, three) on the main-lighted areas.

Establishing the ratio. There are several simple methods of establishing a 3-to-1 ratio. These methods include using:

1. Both the main light and the fill light at equal distances from the subject, with the main light at twice the fill-light intensity. For example, with variable-power electronic flash units, the main light could be used at 200 watt-seconds, with the fill light at 100 watt-seconds.

2. Two identical lights, but with the main light closer to the subject. The specific distance for each light can be determined quickly by thinking of the lens *f*-stop openings as a distance scale. With this system, a 3-to-1 ratio is achieved if the main light is "one stop" closer to the subject than the fill light. For example, if the main-light-to-subject distance is 4 feet, the fill-in light should be placed 5.6 feet from the subject; if the main light is at 8 feet, the fill light should be at 11 feet, and so on.

3. Two identical lights equidistant from the subject, with a diffusing screen over the fill light to reduce its intensity by one-half. Two thicknesses of KODAPAK Sheet, .0075 inch, Matte, or one thickness of spun glass approximately meets this requirement. An exposure meter can, of course, be used to check the amount of light absorbed by the diffusing screen. However, the disadvantage of this method is that the main light is usually undiffused—probably an undesirable situation for general portraiture.

4. An exposure meter. Strobe meters adapted for measuring incident light can be used directly. Reflected-light meters can be used to read the light re-

flected from a test card, such as the KODAK Neutral Test Card, held close to and in front of the subject. Either the gray side or the white side can be used, whichever gives more satisfactory readings at the particular level of illumination under consideration. When the main plus fill-in illumination is read, the incident-light meter or card should be turned to the position which gives the maximum reading. The actual reflectance is not important for this use, because the readings are only comparative and will not be used for exposure determination. All lights should be on if an incident-light meter is used. If a test card is used, any backlights or sidelights which might influence the meter directly should be turned off. When fill-in illumination is read, the incident-light meter or card should be turned toward the camera lens, and the main light should be turned off.

The exposure-meter method for establishing the desired lighting ratio is recommended, since the lights can be used feathered or baffled with barn doors or head screens, thus not inhibiting any desired technique of lighting control for the most artistic effect.

Highlight Brilliance

"Highlight brilliance" usually refers to the degree of specularity of facial highlights. The principles governing this important aspect of facial rendition should be very familiar to portrait photographers. Generally, most photographers strive for an artistic midpoint between the two extremes of rendering a face so that it appears perfectly matte and rendering it with such strong highlights that it appears excessively oily. The desired degree of highlight brilliance is sometimes influenced by local public taste and individual photographic style. However, it should be kept in mind that, up to a point, the more brilliant the facial highlights, the more three-dimensional the rendition becomes. Of course, this effect can be overdone; if so, it is especially unfortunate in color portraiture, because the skin color will then be lost in resulting prints.

Most of the necessary control over highlight brilliance can be provided by a slight lateral movement of either or both the main and the fill-in light. It is

absolutely necessary to appraise this effect from the position of the camera lens, however. If additional controls are needed for certain subjects, they can be furnished by either of the following means:

The first is applying makeup to the subject. Powder can be used to reduce excessive facial reflectivity; cold cream, applied judiciously, to increase highlight brilliance.

The second lies in the lighting. The larger and more diffused the frontal light, the more matte the face will appear; conversely, small and undiffused lights cause the most pronounced highlight brilliance.

As an occasional technique, some photographers use, in addition, a small, undiffused light called a "highlighter," above and in front of the subject's face, to reinforce the highlights by adding to their specular appearance. This light should be fairly weak; it should cause no discernible shadows of its own when used in conjunction with conventional lighting; and it should not be used so far forward as to add additional catchlights to the eyes.

In either black-and-white or color portraiture, beware of obliterating delicate facial highlights by overexposing the negative.

Camera Height for Normal Perspective

One of the most important decisions you make at the outset of a portrait sitting is at what height to place the camera in relation to the subject. A series of factors influences this decision. The first factor is the amount of the figure you are going to include in the photograph: For normal perspective in a head-and-shoulders portrait, place the camera level, with the optical axis of the lens at the height of the subject's lips and tip of the nose. For a three-quarter figure, lower the camera until the center of the lens is level with the upper chest. For a full-length figure, lower the camera again until it is level with, or a little below, the waist. This low position will produce an increased feeling of grace and composure.

Another factor affecting the choice of camera height is the shape of the subject's face and how you would like to influence the way it is rendered. In a head-and-shoulders composition, raise the camera above the center of the face to help elongate the nose, narrow the chin, reduce fullness of the jaws, or broaden the forehead. Lower the camera below the center if you wish to shorten the nose, reduce the width and height of the forehead, or accentuate the chin and neck.

The Illustrations: The accompanying illustrations were made with an 8 x 10 studio camera and a 14-inch lens. The electronic flash lighting was used throughout the series without any adjustment in position or height. The only changes were raising and lowering the camera and refocusing on the eyes.

The model was chosen for the regularity of her features. She was instructed to hold the same head position throughout the series and to focus her eyes on a spot slightly to the right of the camera and at eye level.

As you compare the illustrations, pay particular attention to the shape of the head, length of the nose and neck, and general contour of the figure. Analysis of the series illustrates another factor in choosing the camera height in portraiture. Note the change in lighting effect as the angle of reflection is changed by raising or lowering the camera. Lighting is the means of creating form. Therefore, to produce the most effective portrait, your lighting must be balanced and adjusted in accordance with the camera height chosen for the sitting.

Camera at eye level

3½ inches below

3½ inches above

7 inches below

7 inches above

10 inches below

10 inches above

14 inches below

14 inches above

Corrective Techniques

The successful portrait photographer realizes that his principal aim is to obtain characteristic likenesses of his subjects. At the same time, however, he must temper reality with flattery. The portraitist does this by combining judicious posing, suitable lighting, and appropriate choice of camera angle. Although each situation in portraiture is different from all the others, the following suggestions for corrective treatment are generally accepted.

Difficulty	Suggested Treatment
Prominent forehead	Tilt chin upward Lower camera position
Long nose	Tilt chin upward Face directly toward lens Lower main light Lower camera position
Narrow chin	Tilt chin upward
Baldness	Lower camera position Screen to shield head Use no hair light Blend top of head with background tone
Angular nose	Minimize effect by turning face toward lens
Broad face	Raise camera position Use short lighting Turn face to three-quarter position
Narrow face	Lower main light Use broad lighting
Wrinkled face	Use diffuse lighting Lower main light Use three-quarter pose
Double chin	Raise main light Tilt chin upward Use high camera position
Facial defects	Keep on shadow side
Prominent ears	Hide far ear behind head Keep near ear in shadow Consider profile view
Glasses	Tilt downward by elevating bows slightly Adjust fill light laterally Have subject raise or lower chin slightly Use small light source and etch reflection from negative
Deep-set eyes	Lower main light Use lower lighting ratio
Protruding eyes	Have subject look downward
Heavy-set figure	Use short lighting Use low-key lighting Use dark clothing Vignette shoulders and body Blend body with background tone

Makeup

Today is the era of the natural look in portraiture. This does not mean, however, that a touch of makeup, properly applied before the sitting, will not greatly enhance the final photographic result. In fact, a few minutes' time at the makeup table can often make the difference between a successful sitting and a retake. In any case, skillful makeup pays for itself in retouching saved.

Usually, normal street makeup is sufficient for most female subjects, providing it has been properly applied. The following notes and accompanying illustrations may help those who are unsure of the art of makeup.

Makeup of a color near your subject's own skin tone, lightly applied, most often gives best results. A soft, becoming hairdo and comfortable clothes, sports or dressy, promote a feeling of self-confidence in your model as she faces the camera. Keep the hair soft, clean, and shiny. Teasing is out and excessive hair spray gives a tacky appearance. If the hair has been set recently, brush it out thoroughly. Keep an eye out for stray wisps and misplaced locks throughout the sitting.

Choosing the costume for the sitting is an important task and one that should be discussed beforehand. Advise your subject to stick to simple styles, avoiding bold prints, large bows, and other features that will distract from the face. Suggest a color or colors that are soft and becoming. A round neckline is a poor choice for a round face; a V-neck is slimming. Avoid sleeveless dresses for older women. The flesh of the upper arm loosens with age and appears sagging and heavy in photos. (When arms and hands appear in a portrait, they should be made up.) Suggest long sleeves and heavier fabrics to help fill out a too thin person. Light colors will add weight, too.

If you are going to apply makeup from scratch, the skin must first be thoroughly cleansed. Then apply a thin coat of base the same color as the skin. This will give the skin a smooth even tone, but should not change its color.

Eyes are the focal point of any portrait and should be given careful atten-

tion. Before starting eye makeup, use decongestant-type eyedrops to eliminate redness. Reduce prominent eyebrow bones by using gray eye shadow directly under the eyebrow. Use pale eye shadow of neutral shades on the upper lids. (A mixture of half white makeup base and half neutral base is a good combination.) Mascara will contrast the lashes against the pale eye shadow, making them look both longer and darker. Use black mascara for brunettes and warm brown for blondes and redheads. Use false lashes only if absolutely necessary and put mascara on the natural lashes before attaching the false ones. Avoid heavy eyebrow pencil. An ordinary, soft news-writer pencil can be used to extend the eyebrows or to fill in any thin spaces. Brush the brows first, keeping them in a soft curve without pointed corners. Avoid dark, thick eyeliner above or below the eyes. Eyeliner color should match that of the mascara. A *thin* line on the upper lid will enlarge the eye. Use no line on the bottom lid. Eyeliner is especially flattering to the girl wearing glasses.

A touch of cream rouge on the cheek bone, blended up and out toward the scalp, may be necessary for that glowing look. Next, pat on very lightly—do not rub—a coat of translucent powder and brush off any excess. This will set the makeup to last for a long period of time. Excessive powder produces a dull, flat appearance. Some sheen or luster on the bridge of the nose and the cheekbone adds roundness to the face.

Light, warm shades of lipstick photograph most naturally. If the lips have sufficient natural color, a light coat of gloss will provide highlights.

In photographing small children, consider applying a touch of lip gloss, and in some cases a touch of blush to the cheeks. It will often enhance the appearance of the subjects and give them a healthy look.

Complexion flaws, blemishes, and scars should be compensated for by coloring, not heavy covering. Ruddy skin can be subdued and brown spots can be evened out by carefully applying a lighter makeup base directly to the area with a brush. Later, cover the entire face with a light application of base that is the color of the normal flesh. Try to

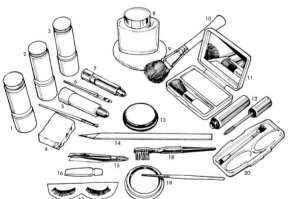

1	White Base	**11**	Blush and Brush
2	Natural Base	**12**	Mascara
3	Medium Base	**13**	Rouge
4	Make-Up Sponge	**14**	Eyebrow Pencil
5	Eyebrow Shadow	**15**	Tweezers
6	Lip Brush	**16**	Glue
7	Lipstick	**17**	False Lashes
8	Translucent Powder	**18**	Brow Brush
9	Powder Puff	**19**	Eyeliner and Brush
10	Powder Brush	**20**	Eyelid Shadow

maintain the subject's natural skin tone. It may be necessary to mix several colors of makeup base, but the results are worth the trouble. To improve sallow skin, add slight tones of pink in the form of translucent gel or cream blush. To reduce the prominence of flesh under the jaw, tone it with a slightly darker shade of base. As a general rule, use a base slightly lighter than skin tone to bring out a facial feature and a darker one to make it recede into surrounding tones.

A male subject should have at least a week-old haircut. A fresh haircut has sharp lines and gives an almost bald appearance. He should be freshly shaven, for the slightest beard will show. Control reflections from bald heads by screening the main light. Receding hairlines (which photography accentuates by about a half-inch) can be helped by blending a little blush very carefully

1 Completely cleansed face (stick cleanser)

2 Lightener under the eye (right side)

3 Base on one-half face (right side)

7 Mascara—on right eye

8 Mascara on left eye—false lash on right eye

9 Eye liner applied with fine line

13 Translucent powder being applied

along and into the hairline. For excessively oily skin, a very light touch of translucent powder can be used to reduce reflections. Brush off any excess. However, shiny skin is more acceptable in portraits of men than of women. Blemishes and other defects in male subjects can be treated with the same type of corrective makeup as used with female subjects.

In all uses of makeup, remember to keep that natural look. A little time spent at the makeup table may save hours at the retouching desk.

4 Eye shadow applied to eyebrow bone

5 Mixture—one-half base and one-half white for eyelid

6 Eyelid shadow applied (right side)

10 Penciling eyebrow

11 Cream rouge (right side)

12 Rouge applied (right side). Position of spotting rouge (left side)

14 Addition of dry powder blush

15 Lipstick applied with brush

16 Face completely made up

Outdoor Portraiture

"What's so hard about taking pictures of people outdoors? Everybody does it. Why pay a professional photographer for pictures that require no lights, no studio, and no set?" These are the questions that may come to the minds of some prospective customers if you suggest this type of portraiture to them. Actually, they are good questions. And a professional portrait photographer must be prepared to demonstrate some very good answers in order to survive.

Here are a few examples of successful outdoor portraiture. Notice that the sun is usually backlighting or sidelighting the subject, with flash units or reflectors adding the proper fill-in illumination. Outdoor portrait lighting, necessarily, is quite fundamental.

Success in this type of work lies in selecting a relevant background, setting a mood by pose or activity, and finally, directing viewer attention by selective focus, print manipulation, and cropping.

Because of a growing awareness and appreciation of nature, the field of outdoor portraiture will continue to grow. Take every opportunity to engage in this pleasant endeavor, but remember that it requires all of the sensitivity and professional know-how of studio work.

Outdoor Fill-Lighting

One of the qualities that separates the professional portrait from the snapshot is the proper maintenance of a reasonable lighting ratio. This is particularly true in outdoor portraiture, where the main light is quite unadjustable.

By reasonable lighting ratio we mean something between 1 to 2 and 1 to 6; that is, where the light on the shadow side is from 1/2 to 1/6 that on the highlight side, as measured by a reflection light meter.

There are two methods of providing the fill source with which to maintain this lighting ratio: The first and simplest is to use large reflectors. You can make adequate flat reflectors from 20 by 24-inch double-weight mounting board, with one side white and the other covered with matte aluminum foil that has been crumpled and reflattened. Don't use mirror-finished foil, as it pro-

Family Group on the Riverbank

Outdoor work is always exciting. There is more space to discover workable subject relationships. The challenge is to bring composition, light, continuity of subject matter, and family relationships together in a decorative way. A task that is not always easily accomplished.

Generally, early morning or late afternoon is considered best for lighting. However, beautiful light can be found any time of the day. It becomes a function of composition.

This group portrait, made just before sunset, has the mood of that time of day: warm sun, quiet water, and soft shadows. It is a picture different from anything anyone else will ever have, because that particular time on the river is gone.

Studio work may become repetitious—outdoor work is more easily individual.

A 100-watt-second, battery-powered electronic flash unit filled the shadows cast by the sun 5 minutes before sunset. A 4 x 5-inch view camera and a 7½-inch lens were used to expose *Kodak Ektachrome* Film 6115, Daylight Type. From the original transparency, dye transfer prints were made for delivery.

duces specular reflections and hot spots. Use the matte aluminum side when you need a fairly strong fill and the white side for a soft glow. Regardless of the reflector, base your exposure on the fill-light intensity.

The other method of fill-lighting is to use electronic flash. Compute the exposure as follows:

1. Place your subject with his back or side to the sun.

2. Check on the table below to find the distance range from subject to flash for proper fill-in. Read to the right on the BCPS rating line for your electronic flash unit. You will get full fill (1-to-2 lighting ratio) when the subject is at the near distances, average fill (1-to-3 lighting ratio) when the subject is at the middle distances, and slight fill (1-to-6 lighting ratio) when the subject is at the far distances shown in the table.

3. Adjust your camera shutter to the speed recommended for the subject distance/lighting ratio that you select from the table. Then, using an exposure meter, determine the correct lens opening to be used for your frontlighted subject in daylight at the shutter speed selected.

4. Set your lens opening and expose the picture.

This table works for any film because it is based on the ratio of flash to sunlight, not on the film speed.

Subject Distances for Fill-In Flash with Electronic Flash (Distance in Feet)

Output of Unit BCPS	Shutter Speed with X Synchronization*				
	1/25-1/30	1/50-1/60	1/100-1/125	1/200-1/250	1/400-1/500
350	1½-2-3½	2-3-4½	3-4-7	3½-5-8	4½-6-10
500	2-3-4	2½-3½-5½	3½-5-8	4-5½-9	5½-8-13
700	2-3-4½	2½-3½-6	4-5½-9	4½-6-10	6½-9-15
1000	2½-3½-5½	3½-5-8	5-7-11	6-8-13	8-11-18
1400	3-4-7	4-5½-9	6-8-13	7-10-15	9-13-20
2000	3½-5-8	5-7-11	7-10-15	8-11-18	11-15-25
2800	4-5½-10	6-8-13	8-11-18	10-14-20	13-18-30
4000	5-7-11	7-10-15	10-14-20	12-17-25	15-21-35
5600	6-8-13	8-11-18	12-17-25	15-21-30	18-25-40
8000	7-10-15	10-14-20	15-21-30	17-24-40	20-28-50

*With focal-plane shutters, use the shutter speed that your camera manual recommends for electronic flash.

Couple in Wheat Field ▶

The couple wanted a casual, but unusual, picture featuring the ring as an announcement of their intention to marry. This soft, warm, engagement portrait is the result. No artificial light is necessary, for the ripening wheat itself reflects adequate illumination to fill the shadows. The selective softness of focus is arranged by photographing through a sheet of clear glass, partially smeared with petroleum jelly. The pose, with downcast eyes, eliminates the subjects' tendency to squint in the full sunlight.

Girl and Horse

In outdoor portraiture, when does a photograph stop being a portrait and become a landscape? In this picture of a young girl and her prized pet, careful printing-down of the surrounding foliage effectively directs attention to the subject and avoids pictorialism.
The position of the horse (head down) makes this a portrait of a girl with a horse, not a portrait of a horse with a girl.

The lighting is completely natural and without artificial fill.

Mother and Sons

Begin with the idea or concept, then find the situation that will best convey the feeling you wish to project. Finally, motivate the pose, mood, and expression to produce the pictorial statement. This picture of a young mother, telling a story to her boys in the cool shade of the forest, is a fine example of preplanning and follow-through in outdoor portraiture.

The lighting is entirely natural. No additional fill light is necessary. The camera is a Hasselblad camera, set at 1/30 sec at f/4 (wide open). *Kodacolor-X* Film is the choice of negative material for two reasons—its wide exposure latitude and its great resolving power. There is no problem making excellent 30 x 40-inch prints from properly exposed negatives.

Couple in Woods

For this late-afternoon portrait of a young couple, there is enough skylight left to fill in the shadow detail nicely. The setting sun rim-lights the subjects as it sends long, warm highlights across the forest floor. The color balance of the print is intentionally on the orange-yellow side, to prevent cold flesh tones and to project the feeling of late summer.

Unusual Portrait Techniques and Presentations

You may not like the pictures in this chapter. You may like some of them and hate others. You may even wonder how a professional photographer could have the nerve to sell a bunch of darkroom tricks as a portrait. Back at the beginning of this book, we quoted both Leonardo da Vinci and Paul L. Anderson to the effect that a portrait is, among other things, descriptive of the sitter's personality. Here, certainly, are personality descriptions far beyond the scope of any conventional photograph. The devices used to produce these psychological descriptions are not new—double exposure, double printing, posterization, projection, texture screens—all are adapted from the discoveries made in the era of early black-and-white photography. These discoveries have simply been applied to modern color photography, but carefully and selectively applied by the photographer to characterize his sitter. These portraits are not haphazard pictures. They represent many hours of darkroom work and a complete knowledge of color theory as well as considerable insight into human nature. What is more, they sell!

Study these photographs and the methods that were used to accomplish them. Accept or reject them as ideas for your own use as you see fit. Use them as a springboard for your own original concepts, too.(That goes for all the posing and lighting ideas throughout this book.) Then, as you produce your own portraits, try a new technique on an appropriate subject. If you succeed in doing something out of the ordinary in one of ten sittings, or one of twenty-five sittings, or even one of one hundred sittings, you will be growing as a modern portrait photographer. As you grow artistically, so will your reputation and your business. And so will your pleasure in your chosen field.

Photo-Posterization

Posterization, the reduction of a continuous-tone picture to a limited number of flat tones, is an effective way to add excitement, characterization, and design to portraits. It is a powerful technique, and therefore not appropriate for all subjects.

Here is a successful use of the simplest form of photo-posterization. This two-tone portrait was originally exposed on *Kodak Tri-X* Pan Film 120. A series of exposures onto high-contrast film produced a variety of black-and-white transparencies. One of these was chosen as most suitable and a contact negative was made, again on high-contrast film. That negative was retouched and printed to produce this strong portrait.

To add color to a posterization, the process has to be carried two steps further. A series of tonal-separation positives was produced from the continuous-tone negative of the young girl by successive exposures on high-contrast film. These positives were then exposed onto sheets of positive-printing color diazo material. Finally, the sheets were registered to produce the multicolored transparency.

Posterization techniques are described in Kodak Pamphlet No. E-93, *Photo-Posterization*. Single copies are available without charge from Department 412-L, Eastman Kodak Company, Rochester, N.Y. 14650.

Double Exposure

Double-exposure portraits are being offered as a regular part of the portrait line of many professional studios.

Two separate photographic arrangements are used to produce the result. Great care must be taken to fit one exposure into appropriate areas of the other. A clear acetate overlay on the ground glass, marked with each composition, helps to prevent any overlap of images. In the outdoor example, a black focusing cloth was held behind the boy's head in the close-up segment to eliminate background exposure. Then, for the second segment, the dark green hillside was positioned in the area of the face. In the studio shots, carefully controlled lighting provided the areas of little or no illumination necessary in each setup.

Since these double photographs are made on *Kodak Ektacolor* Film, manipulations such as retouching, burning-in and dodging during printing, and print retouching, are easily made in order to enhance the final product.

Blurred Bride

A feeling of movement and unreality is projected by this unusual bridal portrait. The situation is a normal one. The bride is walking toward an open door through which daylight illuminates the scene. The groom stands beside the door, looking at his new wife.

The special effects of color and blur are added by two 6-inch-square, colored gels taped into a cone in front of the lens. The gel colors are magenta and deep orange. On the side of the lens toward the light source, the magenta gel transmits the colored image of the groom. On the side of the lens away from the light source, the orange gel reflects a distorted image of the bride's white gown without changing its color. When using colored filter material in this manner, you must adjust the cone each time to fit the subject. Black masking tape to hold the cone is indispensable in this case, as in so many others, because it holds tightly and is reflection-free.

Daisy Girl

This dreamlike portrait has the appearance of a double exposure, but was actually taken through a double imaging lens designed and fabricated by the photographer.

The single-source butterfly lighting gives a natural outdoors feeling, while the huge flower images and the pensive expression of the subject add an unworldly quality.

Projections

The same subject—two different treatments. A 2¼-inch-square transparency of a beautiful girl, projected into rim-lighted, cupped hands, produces a portrait into which many meanings can be read. Note how the shape of the face is accented by the lines of the man's palms.

When rear-projected onto textured plastic sheeting, the same transparency produces an eerie underwater feeling, with swirling highlights and deep shadows.

In both instances, the projected image is recorded on 35mm *Kodak* High Speed *Ektachrome* Film (Tungsten).

Mezzotint Posterization

A kiss on the forhead is a delicate and traditional expression of love. To soften and mute
the colors, and to follow in the romantic style of the impressionist artists of the 19th century,
a mezzotint screen is used. This screen breaks tonal areas into tiny dots of color surrounded by
white, effectively desaturating the usually intense posterization effect.

A color transparency came first, then tonal separations on high-contrast film. Next came a
number of contact prints on diazo sheets of various hues through a series of mezzotint screens.
The resulting color transparency was copied on *Kodak Ektacolor* Internegative Film 6110
and printed to size for reproduction.

Soft-Focus Portrait

This photograph is concerned with depicting the flowing, radiant beauty of the subject in a special way. The lens is one designed by the photographer, using elements of a 16mm zoom lens modified to cover a 35mm format.

The lighting consists of a soft main light to the right of the camera and a strong kicker light directly behind the subject's head. This backlight causes a great amount of flare in the soft-focus lens, diffusing the image and enhancing the beauty of the girl in a manner that no high-resolution lens could.

Fire and Ice

A swirl of red, yellow, and orange color emphasizes a passionate and direct personality. The highly lighted background consists of sheets of red and yellow acetate. The color is repeated in the foreground by means of a reflection from a clear acetate sheet held between the lens and the subject. The acetate sheet is manipulated until the desired reflection is observed in the viewfinder.

The camera is a 35mm single-lens reflex. The film is *Kodak* High Speed *Ektachrome* Film (Tungsten).

Diamond Moiré

This psychedelic portrait is the result of a double duplication. The camera original is a conventional portrait on *Kodak* High Speed *Ektachrome* Film 120. The double moiré pattern is from two negative images of a circular moiré design purchased from Edmund Scientific Co., 300 Edscorp Building, Barrington, N.J. 08007. (The Edmund Catalog contains hundreds of scientific and optical items applicable to photographic experimentation.)

To produce this result, the portrait was first duplicated onto *Kodak Ektachrome-X* Film 135, using a conventional slide-duplicating stand. Then the negatives of the moiré pattern were positioned on the stand so that the convergence of the patterns centered on the eyes of the subject. The portrait transparency was then removed from the copy stand and a second exposure made through a yellow filter.

Face with Spiral Moiré ▶

This picture starts with all attention on the subject's eye. Psychologically, the pattern seems to refer only to her gaze. But as the spiral expands, it delineates her forehead, the curved plane under her eye, her nose, and her jawline. The spiral reverses itself to fill in the dark area of her hair and finally is lost in the dark surround. So after the strong circular pattern attracts the viewer to her eye, it eventually defines her entire face.

The photograph was initially shot with black-and-white film. Tone separations were made on high-contrast film and contact-printed onto color-diazo material through a spiral-pattern negative. The spiral negative was rotated slightly or reversed between exposures. The final transparency consists of 8 layers of material.